A
DENTON HOLME
CHILDHOOD

by

Babs Cullen

© Edith Bell Gubbins 1994
First Published in the United Kingdom, 1994
By Richard Stenlake, Ochiltree Sawmill, The Lade, Ochiltree, Ayrshire KA18 2NX
Telephone: 01290 700266

ISBN 1-872074-45-6

DEDICATION

To my dear friend, Ashley.

FOREWORD

All my childhood memories going back to the late Twenties and into the Thirties, particularly of my life in one of Carlisle's best known districts, Denton Holme, have sufficiently stimulated me to put these to paper. It would, I feel, be somewhat of a waste not to record these fragments from the past, the joys and tribulations of what that life portrayed and actually happened.

My beloved brothers Hylton, Bill and I grew up listening repeatedly to our dear mother and father's accounts of how they met and eventually married and how they came to live in Denton Holme. These fascinating tales were told to us over and over again, so much so, that they were vividly imprinted upon our minds, never ever to be forgotten.

What I am about to write is word for word perfectly authentic and, were my darling brothers alive today I know that they would wholeheartedly endorse my sentiments.

Chapter One

The Hand of Fate

As in all stories there has to be a beginning. I can therefore think of no nicer way than to commence, in the main, with my dearly beloved parents.

The First World War had just ended, and immediately after being demobilised from the Army, my Dad, George, and his brother Dick joined their father, George Cullen Senior in the family butcher's business in Carlisle's covered Market. Mother, on the other hand, worked further down the market with her mother, Sarah Hodson, selling fruit, vegetables and confectionery.

At the time, this vast building of Victorian origin, created its own particular charm with its crescent shaped row of shambles where all the butchers conducted their business. According to Mother, one only had to stand still and look right over the tops of the many stalls to appreciate the beauty and colour of the many varieties of fruits and exquisite array of flowers. Inevitably, much joy and pleasure was given to the many local shoppers both young and old, and it never failed to delight visitors to the City.

Now trade was good for the Hodsons, in fact it was very good! Grandmother and Mother had a most pleasing personality and, together with a well stocked stall of top quality produce, record sales were constantly evident.

Without doubt, their thrift and go-ahead attitude were to be admired and Grandmother would carefully invest much of the well-earned profits into several properties in and around Carlisle. Her policy was to be a lady of independent means in her advancing years, plus, of course, to eventually leave Mother financially secure.

Being exceedingly pretty, Mother's very dark hair and most beautiful expressive brown eyes and wonderful country-fresh complexion could attract many a keen eligible bachelor. Come-what-may, however many times these young admirers would frequent the stall and no matter how much money they'd spend in the process, their charm and advances were to no avail. Not one of them enamoured her in the slightest, but, of course, she hadn't yet encountered Dad had she!

Fate was to take a hand, when one morning as Dad was walking through the market he caught sight of Mother as she was busily polishing the large brass weighing scales. This was seemingly her first chore of the day after removing all the protective covers from the stall. Grandmother, you see, was an extremely particular lady, and her so-called tools of the trade had to be absolutely spick and span in readiness for the day's business.

Mother so often used to relate her first meeting with Dad and, with great affection, said that he was extremely polite and had a most refreshing approach. His name, he said, was George Cullen, and explained that he had just returned from the Army to join his father in the family business at the top end of the market.

Mother likewise introduced herself, telling him that her name was Edith. She explained her situation as she pointed towards the large green and gold sign which dominated the stall, that S. Holden, Sarah, was in fact her mother.

They chatted amicably for some minutes and an instant rapport was struck between them. Addresses were exchanged. Mother lived at No. 6 Etterby Terrace, Stanwix, a suburb to the North of the City, whilst Dad lived at The Near Boot Inn, Whiteclosegate, which was a couple of miles or so further on. His brother Dick and sisters Bess, Nan and Clara also lived there, and his mother, he told her, ran the pub, whilst his father attended to the business in the market.

Before departing Dad purchased from her a bag of pears. These, he told her, were his favourite fruit. He looked into her lovely eyes and, as though his soul had been set on fire with a deep instant love, warmly shook her by the hand and walked away.

From that day forward, Mother was constantly haunted by Dad's presence, and furthermore, no customer bought more pears than he!

Over the ensuing weeks, it was quite apparent that Dad was totally lovesmitten, and nothing in the world could prevent him from staying away from Mother. Subsequently slight discord between Grandfather Cullen and he quickly prevailed as a consequence of his frequent absence from the business! In his defence, Dad was quick to point out the extremely long hours he worked, and felt entitled to a little respite, especially to see his beloved Edie!

Mother and Dad continued with their courtship and, after fifteen months of constantly seeing each other, the inevitable happened. Dad popped the question!

Realising that this was such an important stepping-stone in her life, and despite the fact that she adored Dad, Mother decided to mull over her future prospects very carefully before finally accepting his proposal.

The thought of acquiring three sisters-in-law, plus a brother-in-law and, of course, a father and mother-in-law, was quite daunting and was to be viewed with much trepidation. Mother, being of a timorous nature, wondered above all else if she would be really happy.

The matter, Grandmother Hodson decided, would have to be discussed in great depth that very evening, but the afternoon, she pointed out, belonged to her and her alone! She apparently took leave from the stall to indulge herself in a little frivolity, which was to take to the skies in an aeroplane with the well-known Sir Alan Cobham. The event, I would add, did not pass without Mother having a few anxious moments! I believe the fare to be flown over Carlisle was about five shillings a time.

Although Grandmother was hard-working as well as an astute businesswoman, she always believed that life was to be enjoyed, and such a golden opportunity as this, she decided, was not to be allowed to pass her by.

Her photograph was taken in the aeroplane before take-off, to mark this momentous occasion, on the back of which she wrote, 'To Edie, With Love, Mother. Flew over Carlisle, February 11th, 1920.'

With both feet firmly on the ground again, Grandmother spent the evening discussing Mother's future. Dad's many attributes scored highly in her estimation, pointing out that there were few young men who would have left home at the age of sixteen in order to join the Army and endure those horrific years in France. His courage, she said, was to be greatly admired and respected. His determination to be a successful businessman, plus his impeccable manners, also went a long way in Grandmother's estimation.

Mother sat there absorbing every word!

Now Grandmother, who was a Miss Sarah Bell before her marriage, and who seemed to be brought up on quotations, couldn't help but refer to one of her favourites of that moment which she thought most appropriate.

'And remember this, Edie', she said, 'you always get the button to match the cloth!'

After giving the matter a great deal of deliberation and inwardly digesting Grandmother's persuasive comments, Mother decided to accept her beloved George's offer of marriage.

Dad was positively jubilant that he had won the hand of his darling Edie, his priceless pearl, and so, after much careful preparation, the wedding subsequently took place at St. Michael's Church, Stanwix, on the 10th August, 1920.

Edith May Hodson, who was regarded by many as one of the most beautiful brides of her day, became Mrs. George William Cullen.

This moment is appropriate to mention that several years ago when visiting a very dear friend of mine, she introduced me to her gardener, a gentleman of advancing years. His name was Mr. Little. We sat having a cup of tea, when the old gentleman referred to Mother, saying how he vividly remembered, as a boy of ten, delivering milk to her home in Etterby Terrace. It was, in fact, some extra milk which he had forgotten to leave earlier that morning. The front door opened as he walked along the short path, when out came Mother, the most beautiful bride he had ever seen. He explained how he just stood there absolutely spellbound in admiration of her, adding with a smile that it was so unusual for him as he had always been regarded as a bit of a tough nut!

He had, he said, seen many brides since those early days, but the vision of my lovely Mother had remained with him all his life.

I was quite overwhelmed and filled with pride as I sat there listening to Mr. Little's kind remarks.

Some memories can, I suppose, fade away with the passing years, whilst others remain in the heart for ever.

Chapter Two

New Beginnings

After their honeymoon, Mother and Dad settled down in a pretty little cottage at Harker, a small village to the North of Carlisle, where they lived for several years. The cottage is still there to this day, but of course has been extensively improved. So primitive were conditions, fresh tap water was not directly available, but, love knowing no boundaries, they would get their daily supply from an old pump which was a quarter of a mile or so away through a thickly wooded area.

Grandmother Hodson, on the other hand, found her new way of life, that of living alone, to be quite unbearable. Her brave words of late, telling Mother that not only the business but her many hobbies would keep her busy, were all to no avail. How she missed her beloved daughter, particularly when sitting by the fire at the end of each day and gazing at the vacant chair.

I remember Mother telling me that when she went to visit Grandmother shortly after returning from her honeymoon, all the portraits of her which had always been so proudly displayed, were turned towards the walls.

She couldn't bear to look at them any more, she told Mother, emotionally admitting that she was not as tough as she thought. Realising, however, that she wouldn't be the first mother to lose a daughter through marriage, that given time to adjust, she was sure she would come to terms with the situation.

Mother was so understanding and put her arms lovingly around Grandmother to comfort her.

They continued to chat over tea and cake, and then at Mother's suggestion, set out some sheet music and each indulged in playing the piano and violin. Grandmother's spirits were uplifted and, if only for a short while, gave her immense pleasure.

Grandmother was the youngest of an exceedingly large family consisting of six brothers and six sisters, all of whom were talented musicians. Her parents, who were of the farming fraternity, were well known throughout the Penrith area. Each member of the family played the violin with great skill and, according to Mother, there were twelve of these most beautiful instruments hanging round the walls of the farmhouse parlour.

The family were all evidently in great demand to entertain with their sweet music at many social gatherings. These occasions were extremely popular, particularly during 'Term Time' when most of the farmers would hire new lads to work for them.

Grandmother used to tell Mother how she would break the family rules from time to time by putting down her violin and take to the floor with many a dashing partner. Her waltzing was magnificent to behold, a talent which I would like to think has been passed down to her grand-daughter!

The family were popularly known in their musical capacity as The Bells of Brackenborough. One can almost visualise this large Victorian family gathered together in their farmhouse parlour, the echoes of their enchanting strings lending an air of elegance and charm, so typical and reminiscent of those distant bygone days.

Mother, I would add, was an extremely accomplished violinist and a most beautiful pianist, a talent no doubt inherited from those magnificent Bells!

Nature, time and patience being the three great physicians, Grandmother eventually got over her loneliness by taking in the odd paying guest, and life once again became meaningful to her.

Dad continued to work in the family business for some time. The days were long and arduous and with no such thing as a proper dinner hour. I always remember him telling me that Grandfather Cullen would regularly stand at the door of the workshop with his gold watch in his hand, and one night in particular, with a pleasing look on his face, he said … 'We've made good time tonight, George!' It was eleven o'clock!

Sheer drudgery was, of course, quite commonplace in those not so far-off days, and all for such a miserable pittance!

Dad made all the Cumberland sausage, blackpuddings and haggis, to name but a few items, as well as doing his share of work in the shamble. Uncle Dick also worked very hard in the business. Strangely enough, according to Dad, Grandfather never did a decent day's work in his life, but adopted more of a supervisory capacity rather than partake of any hard graft! He was, however, meticulous in his ways. At the beginning of each day, every chopper, every knife, would be placed on the proverbial butcher's block in sparkling condition, each in order or size, almost in regimental fashion.

After much deliberation, Dad decided that the time had come for him to branch out on his own. After all, what was ten shillings a week going to do for Mother and himself, and especially when a baby was on the way.

An opportune moment was seized when Grandfather's brother, Joe Cullen, offered him part of his workshop for storage and the making of sausage and other preparations. Together with some money which Mother had saved, he bought a pony and trap, hence he was well and truly launched!

Dad's courage was to be admired, overcoming many obstacles. Although he was so young, he suffered very badly with gout in his feet. This, he vowed, was caused by spending such long periods of time in the water-filled trenches whilst in France. Little did he realise at that time that he would be dogged with this complaint for the rest of his life, and that for several months of each year he would be compelled to use crutches. His misfortune, however, did not deter him from wanting to be a success. He would go all round the countryside each day selling his succulent Cumberland sausage, together with a good selection of beef, pork and lamb.

Trade became quite brisk, perseverance getting its reward. Within a short period of time Dad progressed from the pony and trap to a small van. What more could a young aspiring businessman want? What indeed!

Within a few years the patter of tiny feet had increased threefold. Hylton was the first-born, then came Bill, and lastly myself. Now although I was christened Edith Bell, from the day I was born Mother and Dad called me Babs. What on earth possessed them, I wonder! Like the old saying that mud sticks, then so has the name of Babs!

An opportunity eventually arose for Dad to acquire his Uncle Joe's butcher's shop at the corner of Denton Street and Norfolk Street in Denton Holme. The old chap decided that the time had come to call it a day. Included in the purchase were two houses, one of them being partly situated over the shop, whilst the other was immediately in Norfolk Street.

And so we left our beloved Harker and moved to Denton Holme, much to the disappointment and regret of my dear Mother.

Although she lived at Stanwix at the time of her marriage, Mother was not a native of Carlisle, and had always lived in the country, at Newton Reigny, a small village outside Penrith. For many years she attended Briggs' High School in Penrith, which was situated high up on a hill near the Beacon, a well-known landmark which overlooks the town to this day.

From the open spaces to a thickly populated part of Carlisle was such a contrast for Mother, and the idea of her sharing a somewhat large back yard amongst four other neighbours was so very hard for her to accept. It appeared, however, that there was no option in the matter.

As the weeks went by, Mother came to like the neighbours and found them extremely kind and helpful. There was old Mrs. McKillop and her daughter Madge, who lived at the far end of the yard, then next door to them was an elderly lady, a Miss Robinson, who lived with her brother Billy. They spoke with a beautiful Irish accent. A long narrow lane which led out on to the street, separated Miss Robinson's house from the next one which was occupied by old Annie and Jimmy Blair. Now these two were great characters, but more about them later!

Our immediate neighbours were Bell and Willie Kendal. Willie was related to Dad, a cousin, I believe, and the fact that he had been employed to work in the business, found the closeness particularly convenient.

Mother gradually came to terms with living in town and was loved and respected by all with whom she came in contact, her disposition being sweet and kind at all times. The fact that Denton Holme was a low-lying environment, with its many factories scattered round about, was a constant source of worry to her. With we little ones in mind, she felt, that after living in the country, our health would become impaired with all the unavoidable smoke from these factories, thus polluting the air.

Hylton, Bill and I slowly adapted ourselves to playing in the yard, although Mother confined us to our own corner in order that we didn't upset the neighbours in any way.

The yard I suppose had its own peculiar charm with its neat, tiny cobblestones which covered the whole area. There were three toilets, I remember, and these were scrubbed and swilled out almost every day with Jeyes fluid. In the far corner was a large wash house which contained an enormous boiler and a mangle. Three small zinc baths hung on the whitewashed walls, together with a washing board, plus three or four iron hoops, although I never knew what useful purpose they served, if any.

There was also a monstrous looking wooden object which was called a 'dolly'. This peculiar three footed gadget was held in both hands and lifted up and down in the wash tub to agitate the washing and to ensure that all excess dirt was removed. Turning the huge wheel on the mangle must have been hard graft and would undoubtedly be quite energy draining to its user.

To the side of the wash house door were two oblong wooden boxes which were filled with red geraniums. These were covered with wire mesh, supposedly to protect the flowers from the birds or cats. This lovely splash of colour seemed to complement the cobblestones and gave added character to the yard. In the spring these boxes were filled with beautiful wallflowers.

Mrs. McKillop, in particular, was such a grand old lady, and although she was quite tiny, she was a wiry little dear. I remember she'd be in the wash house very early each Monday morning. She would fill the boiler with water and then start a fire with a few sticks and coal. Getting the water to boiling point took some considerable time, but Mrs. McKillop would never waste a minute. She'd get the zinc baths from the wall and set one of them under the mangle. This was to catch the water when putting the finished washing through the wooden rollers.

Another bath would be filled with water, to which was added Reckitt's Blue. This was supposed to give the whites that extra touch required for perfect results. Finally, the third bath was used to make a starch mixture, chiefly for stiffening tablecloths and sheets.

As soon as the water reached the right temperature and the washing was carefully dropped into the great boiler, the wash house would be instantly filled with billowing steam which would escape through the open door and window.

Although these methods of the weekly wash were quite primitive and without a doubt very hard work, they were also time consuming and could last for several hours of the day. Not only did dear Mrs. McKillop take it all in her stride, but most housewives accepted it as a way of life for, after all, it was the only method known to them in those days.

The old saying 'new house, new baby', was surely true enough! Within a few months a little sister was born. She was christened Annie, and so with four young ones to look after, Mother most certainly had her work set!

One of my earliest memories was peering into a white cot which was in the corner of the living room, and looking at my little sister. I remember distinctly that she had lovely fair hair. Being so young, I didn't realise that she was very poorly, and besides, at such a tender age it wouldn't have meant anything to me. I may at some time have asked Mother and Dad what had happened to her, as I suppose I must have missed her, but there again, I just don't remember.

Very sadly, my little sister died, and she was only thirteen months old. How Mother and Dad must have been so terribly heartbroken.

It is amazing when I look back on Mother's life with four small children. The going must have been very hard for her. Doubtless, of course, there would be many with even larger families, but their lives must have been constant drudgery. Mother always lovingly called us her little steps and stairs!

Hylton was never enamoured of Denton Holme, as he was a true country-loving boy at heart. Grandmother and Grandfather Cullen had by this time vacated The Near Boot Inn and bought a rather splendid house in the nearby village of Houghton, which was called 'Green Lea'. This beautiful dwelling overlooked the village green with its two delightful ponds. At one side of the house was a huge orchard, and at the other, were several outbuildings where Grandfather kept his pony and cart and a few milking cows. At the back of the house was an immense paddock where his many greyhounds would run freely before being settled in their kennels.

This tempted Hylton like bees to a honeypot! He was, in fact, never away from the place. As he grew a little older, Dad bought him a bicycle in order to travel to and fro as he so desired. Bill and I, on the other hand, were quite happy and totally inseparable. We always had a very deep love for each other, and even when he'd play with his friends along the street, I was always allowed to tag on.

Grandfather was a very keen sportsman and was well-known throughout Cumberland for indulging in greyhound coursing. He employed a full-time gardener-cum-handyman by the name of Jack Nicholson, the majority of whose time was taken up with the dogs as they needed to be groomed each day and taken for long walks to keep them in peak condition.

I was seven years of age when Mother taught me to knit, and the first things I made were neckbands for the greyhounds. They were brightly coloured in red and yellow and, although there were many dropped stitches, Grandfather lovingly accepted them, knowing that I had put a lot of effort into making them.

Whilst staying a few days at Green Lea, I remember Grandfather walking into the living room after a day's coursing. He had four of his greyhounds with him, each wearing beautiful navy blue coats all edged in yellow braiding, plus, of course, the knitted neckbands! I remember him telling everyone what a wonderful day he had had with Lordy (Lord Lonsdale) who was also a great enthusiast in the sport. They were great friends and always got together on these occasions. Had I understood at the time what a cruel sport coursing was, I would have put my knitting wool to better use!

Getting back to Denton Holme, I recall to mind the day when Dad had a rather large consignment of printed matter delivered to the shop. They were bright green pamphlets advertising his name in large black letters, including a list of all the delicious varieties of cooked meats which were available for sale over the counter.

I must proudly admit that Dad had great culinary expertise and was surely a true master of his trade. He could produce the most delicious savouries, and the wonderful aroma from the workshop would fill the air to such an extent, that the likes of old Annie and Jimmy Blair would sit with their kitchen door as wide open as possible, just to breathe in and enjoy these tempting smells.

Anyway, getting back to the pamphlets! After much pleading with Dad and Mother, Bill and I were allowed to go round all the streets and distribute a pamphlet to each household. We hastily loaded our somewhat splendid looking wheelbarrow, and off we went! What an adventure! I'm sure we covered a good half of Denton Holme, and it was great fun, especially when peeping through some of the letter boxes!

When I cast my mind back and think of that particular occasion, our mischievous yet harmless indulgence provided us with so much innocent fun and laughter. Had Mother known of our little goings on, I feel sure we would have been severely reprimanded!

On our way back home I vividly remember walking along Nelson Street, when Bill encountered a few of his pals. We were approaching a tall silver lamp-post which had a small narrow flagpole at its top.
'Bet yu can't claym up tu the top an' hing upsayde doon from that pawl'. said one of them to Bill.

'Bet Aa can', he replied, with a determined look on his face.

'Dee it then', they shouted.

Without hesitation, Bill climbed to the top and hung upside down from the pole. Within seconds, the inevitable happened! My beloved brother came crashing to the ground. How I screamed with fright and anxiety when I bent down to pick him up. His pals, of course, were so scared by what had happened, they instantly ran away.

Bill's blood-covered face I will never forget as long as I live, and what a brow! An immediate lump appeared, making him look completely distorted, and there was no doubt about it, he was completely dazed. I helped him into the wheelbarrow and pushed him the rest of the way home, my heart truly breaking. My sobs were so loud that several people opened their front doors to see what the commotion was all about.

'What's the matter, Babsy love?' I recollect one lady enquiring.

'It's Bill', I said, my face wet with tears. 'He's had an accident.' 'Will he die', I cried, 'will he die?'

'No pet', she said kindly. 'Just get him home to your Mam as quickly as you can and she'll make him better.'

Imagine my poor Mother's face when she saw us come home in such a distressed state. She almost fainted at the very sight of Bill's face. He was immediately bathed, and then Mother put a large lump of butter on his battered brow. Very gently she sat him up in an easy chair by the fire, his aching head supported by a soft cushion. A few days off school was ordered by Dr. Cameron, who came to see him instantly. Never again did I ever remember Bill carry out a 'dare'!

If ever we weren't playing in the back yard, Mother always knew exactly where to find us. We would be sitting with old Annie and Jimmy in their kitchen. They were forever arguing with each other and, because of this, Bill and I used to enjoy their exchange of words, hence a few swear words were added to our vocabulary, much to the annoyance of Mother! Both old dears were very broad of speech, and I particularly remember that Annie always referred to Jimmy as 'Blair'.

Bill and I, being at such an impressionable age, could have picked up the dialect so easily, had Mother not kept a close check on us. As time went by, however, Bill in particular could speak like a true native. Mother just gave up in despair!

Annie, poor old dear, suffered from acute asthma, and I was always deeply fascinated by her, sitting over her blackleaded kitchen range on a spindle-back chair with her feet resting on an old brass fender. She would get this powdered substance, place it on a small tin lid, then set it alight until it smouldered. The fumes were then inhaled.

'It loosens the phlegm, bonny lass', she would say. 'Aye, it loosens the phlegm.'

I used to be so sorry for her, as some days she could hardly catch her breath for wheezing and coughing. At the very sight of Bill, of course, she would beam with delight. He seemed to be an instant pick-me-up to her, even though he was forever getting into her black books with his playful mischief. He was, without a doubt, the apple of her eye, but then, who couldn't have loved my beloved Bill!

From as far back as I can remember, I was somehow blessed with being observant. Old Annie's parlour brings back so many memories to me. I found it most fascinating and can still visualise it to this very day.

The room portrayed its own particular humble charm, with its green walls and dark furniture. The old marble mantelpiece was enhanced by a pair of bronze horses which were placed at either end. There was also a pair of porcelain figures which stood on round black plinths and were covered with glass domes.

Strangely enough, all of the things that Annie treasured on her mantelpiece were two extremely large egg shells. These, I remember, were beautifully painted in gold and delicate pastel shades and were placed on two almost saucer-shaped dishes. I suppose she didn't have any egg cups the appropriate size to accommodate them. Bill and I, incidentally, were forever being warned never to touch them as they were so very fragile.

In the centre of the room was an oval shaped table. This was draped with a deep fringed chenille cloth on which rested a large Family Bible. I don't recollect, however, seeing any chairs around the table.

An aspidistra plant sat majestically in a pot on a small bamboo table beside the window, and the lace curtains which hung from a wooden pole seemed to frame this massive array of greenery and somehow blended in with the character of the room which was so typically Victorian.

Although Annie led poor old Jimmy a bit of a life with her constant nagging, I have to say that she was extremely generous of heart. They were not at all well off, and I expect they lived up to every penny of Jimmy's earnings from the Cummersdale Textile Factory where he had worked all his life.

Despite their circumstances, Annie always managed to scrape a copper or two to spend on the stray pigeons which lived on the rooftops. She'd feed them with corn every day, and they'd come flying down into the street by the dozen, many times holding up the passing traffic.

Never will I forget Jimmy's talent for dyeing Pasche eggs. He'd bring home from the factory a few small fragments of beautifully coloured material, which he'd tear into strips about an inch or so in width. These were then carefully wrapped around the fresh eggs and entwined with lots of fine string. Gently, they'd be put into a pan of water to be boiled for a few minutes.

After allowing them to cool in a bowl of cold water, Jimmy would unwrap them and, to enhance their beautiful appearance, he'd rub a tiny piece of lard on them to give them a delicate sheen. They were so enchanting to look at with their dark rich colours, it seemed such a great pity that they had to be cracked and eaten!

Bearing in mind that Jimmy was of retiring age, he had undoubtedly been a tall, good looking man in his youth. I remember seeing in his kitchen a large framed photograph of a football team of which he was a member, and he looked extremely athletic. Indeed the ravages of time had inevitably paid their toll!

As aforementioned, Bill was never out of hot water with Annie. I am reminded of the day when she gave him twopence to go to Mrs. Blaylock's shop to get a couple of fruit teacakes.

'Noo dawn't be lang', she said, 'they're for me and Blair's tea.'

Off he went, and within minutes was sitting outside our shop door, playing on the flagstones with a small tin car.

A little while passed, when an enraged Annie came flying towards Bill, her old shawl thrust nonchalantly round her shoulders.

'Where's me teacakes, yu layle bugger?' 'Blair's waitin' for 'is tea!'

Bill mischievously looked up at her, telling her that Mrs. Blaylock hadn't any left, so he thought he'd buy the car.

Mother instantly apologised and reimbursed Annie, and gave her a couple of savoury ducks to take back home for tea.

And where was I when all this went on? I was climbing up the shop door driving my poor Mother to distraction!

Business continued to thrive for Dad, and his success was well deserved. Although he worked so hard during the day, much of the making up side was done after the shop closed most evenings. A fine window display of his products was therefore always evident the next morning, fresh and tempting to his customers, and would cause a passer-by to stop and gaze at such mouthwatering delicacies.

I shall never forget both our shop windows, especially during the Christmas period. In one window Dad would fill it to capacity with the most wonderful selection of poultry from chickens to geese and turkeys. The other window was especially attractive, which would bring out Dad's artistic flair to its best advantage. In the centre of the display, he would place a pig's head which he had glazed over with a red polony dye. An orange would be placed in the pig's mouth, and to finish this rather charming creation, he would fix a white paper frill round its neck. The rest of the window would be filled with a marvellous selection of pork, giving his customers a wide range from which to choose. Dad always finished his windows with a garnish of fresh parsley to give added attraction.

It seems such a great pity that photographs were not taken of these delightful, festive-looking windows for posterity's sake, instead of keeping the memory of them locked away in my own mind.

One evening Dad had been making a batch of blackpuddings, and, having a surplus of blood and diced fat simply because he had run out of skins, asked Bill to go across the yard to Annie's and see if she would like some of it for herself and Jimmy. I, of course, had to go as well!

We scampered across the old cobblestoned yard and walked straight into Annie's kitchen. We never used to knock as she was so used to us. Throwing ourselves onto her worn and tattered horse-hair couch, our feet flying in the air, as children do, Billy duly delivered the message.

'Dad wants to knaw if yud layke some black puddin' mixture,' he said with a mischievous smile.

'Eeh, yis bonny lad, A'd luv some', she replied, looking at him so lovingly.

'Just a minute', she continued, 'A'll git yu me raustin' tin.'

She thereupon opened the oven door of the old kitchen range, when out jumped Darky, her big black cat.

'Ere yu are son', she said, handing him the tin.

'But Annie', said Bill in utter amazement, 'aren't yu ganna wesh it oot?'

'Naw, A'm nut', she replied, 'Anywez, Darky's awnly been sleepun' in it and she's clean enough'.

I sat there watching and listening in silence, and the expression on my brother's face will live with me for ever.

'Yu durrty auld bugger', he shouted. 'Nee wunder auld Jimmy's nivver weel, yu'll be poisonin' the poor bugger wid yer muck, poor divvel!'

Well, we jumped up from her couch and neither of us could get out of her kitchen fast enough!

'Git oot yu bloody layle warrlick', she screamed, taking off one of her shoes and throwing it towards Bill.

We literally flew back across the yard, and Dad, seeing the funny side, couldn't help but laugh when we told him what had happened.

I must conclude on this comical episode by saying that Annie eventually got her blackpudding mixture. Dad took it across for her in a large scoop and poured it into the said roasting tin, also apologising for Bill's rudeness to her. All ended happily, Annie telling Dad that although Bill was a 'layle divvel', she simply doted on him.

'Aa luv iv'ry 'air in that lad's 'eed, Geordie', she said.

Before proceeding any further, I would like to remain a little longer on the subject of the aforementioned delicacy! A competition was being held in Hylton's class at Morley Street School, for the best piece of rhyme, only one verse, short and to the point, about any item of food. The pupil with the best effort was to receive the coveted prize of sixpence. Gosh ... sixpence! Hylton immediately thought of Dad's blackpuddings, and so he set to work with great gusto in an attempt to win the prize. His spicy rendition acclaimed him the winner by his teacher, and he was duly presented with the sixpence.

What a wonderful day in the life of an aspiring young poet! He ran all the way home to show us his great prize money and, without a moment to spare, dashed to Robinson's Post Office along Denton Street to purchase a savings stamp.

He was always thrifty for one so young.

Without any further ado, here is Master Hylton George Cullen's 'pièce de résistance'!

CULLEN'S BLACKPUDDINGS
Cullen's blackpuddings are the best –
You can eat them for your belly or your chest!
If you eat them twice a week, you'll hear your belly squeak –
Cullen's blackpuddings are the best!

Speaking of Hylton's thrift, he was by no means greedy, but was always sparing – an idiosyncrasy perhaps to be found in older people. I would like to refer to a case in point!

One Saturday afternoon Mother allowed the three of us to go to the matinee at the Star Picture House which was further along the street. It was a cowboy film. Hylton, being the eldest, was in charge of the money to pay for the seats, and Mother gave him an extra copper or two to buy some sweets. Well, like all children, Bill and I could hardly wait to get sat down, we were so eager to get started on the toffees or whatever Hylton had chosen.

'Pass the goodies, Hylton', said Bill. We both sat with hands outstretched, but to our utter dismay an Oxo cube was thrust into our hands!

'Watt's aw this?,' exclaimed Bill. 'A bloody Oxo cube! Tek a look at aw oor pals, they're aw chewun' goodies!'

'Be quiet', retorted Hylton. 'It'll do you more good than rubbishy sweets.'

I don't propose to add any further comments from Bill, but doubtless one could imagine the atmosphere was somewhat rife for the rest of the afternoon, the fact remaining that, as far as Hylton was concerned, a precious penny or two was saved!

The Star Picture House, incidentally, was a perfect haven, particularly for children attending the Saturday afternoon matinees. Sometimes the queue for admittance would stretch the full length of the Arcade and into the street. The longer the queue, of course, the more it pleased the Manager, Mr. Whalley, a short, extremely rotund gentleman, who would pace up and down to keep his young and over-enthusiastic customers in order!

Mrs Rene George was the lady in charge of the Box Office, whilst her husband played the piano particularly during the intervals.

Each time a certain tune was played, a dog by the name of Spot, and who belonged to the parents of Carlisle's best loved dance teacher, Rita Irving, would run like the wind down the Arcade and invade the picture house. The rascal would then hastily jump onto the stage and bark its head off!

Trying to remove the offending intruder and cast it out forthwith was not a simple task! Spot would cunningly jump from the stage and scurry to the back of the audience and proceed to dodge up and down the various rows of seats. What a fiasco! Over-excitement would then prevail, and the young audience would start throwing all sorts of missiles, simply anything from their pockets like old chestnuts on bits of string to bits of stale chewing gum. How exasperated and hoarse the Manager must have been, trying to control such a mass of vigorous youngsters!

When all was back to normal and the big film about to start, each and every one of us would proceed to stamp our feet on the old knotted wooden floor in eager anticipation. Gosh, Tom Mix! What a hero!!

Were these then the good old, bad old days? To me and my darling brothers, particularly Bill, they were simply wonderful!

Chapter Three

The Magic of Denton Street

Denton Street, which featured a profusion of interesting shops, never failed to have a bright, bustling atmosphere. Each shopkeeper would take a personal interest in his or her customers and, without a doubt, the secret ingredient of their success was courtesy, with the ultimate aim to please and satisfy. Such were those wonderful days!

I remember with great affection one of Denton Street's most outstanding colourful characters, the one and only Mary Ann Bowes who ran a greengrocery business. She was assisted by her aged mother, a small but well-endowed lady who worked extremely hard like an old war horse. Mary Ann, on the other hand, was rather tall, with a somewhat leaner frame than that of her mother. Her thick brown greying hair, which was extremely frizzy, seemed to complement her fresh complexion and large blue eyes. Now no-one was gifted with a greater sense of humour and bubbling personality than she. Her sales patter was so remarkable, and she could have sold rice to a Chinaman!

The premises had a particularly long frontage, thus enabling Mary Ann to display her fruit, vegetables and flowers to great advantage. This she did with great aplomb. All and sundry were given pleasure and delight viewing such artistry, the mixing of colours in just the right places, producing a perfect picture, which could almost have been compared to the beauty of a rainbow.

Inside the shop each shelf would be filled to capacity with a conglomeration of tinned foods, a variety of spices, bottles of sauces, jams and chutneys. Packets of Wild Woodbine cigarettes were also in evidence. Hanging from the old ceiling on large hooks were numerous bunches of dried sage which gave out a wonderful herbal aroma. She even sold her own making of gingerbread which would be cut up into squares and sold for a penny apiece. How she ever found time to bake, however, was beyond one's comprehension, as her shop was always open till late each night. This, of course, was quite the norm in those days.

According to a very dear elderly cousin of mine, Mary Ann did a roaring trade in the sale of 'pot herbs'. These consisted of a cabbage, a turnip, a couple of good sized carrots, including a pinch of thyme, all for the price of twopence. How truly amazing, and somehow deliciously charming! Even the ropes which were bound round the orange boxes would fetch a penny each, and these would be sold mainly to little girls to indulge in the game of skipping. When I think of it, such simple pleasures were derived from a length of rope!

Mary Ann was exceedingly hard-working, but winter time would habitually play havoc with her health. A hot water bottle was always in evidence on her person, which was supported by a thick woollen scarf tied around her waist. There were many times when she looked so ill and full of cold, and a week or so in bed would have done her no harm, but, being so determined to keep going, she ignored her drawbacks. I am told that she died of pneumonia some years ago.

Each encounter with dear Mary Ann was most surely a golden moment to be savoured, for her entertaining wit was truly unique. Indeed, cherished memories of this delightful character, who played such a prominent part in the everyday lives of the community, will always remain lovingly locked away in the archives of my heart and treasured like a pearl beyond price.

There were two particular outfitters shops that I can bring to mind, and these were owned by Mr and Mrs Kay, who, together with the help of their most elegant daughters, did a thriving trade.

Mr Kay, who looked after the gentlemen's and boyswear shop, was particularly renowned for his excellent line in poplin striped shirts, as they were extremely hard-wearing and long-lasting. These, of course, were always in wide appeal to the older generation. Mrs Kay and her daughters, on the other hand, attended to the ladies and girlswear shop which was situated on the other side of the street. Their shop was always exceedingly well stocked from grandmama's winceyette nightgowns to young ladies' dresses and underwear.

With the excitement of Spring in the air, one could always guarantee the Kays producing the most wonderful window displays in time for Easter. This was always a most important time of the year when children were rigged out with new clothes, hence a fine selection was always pleasing to the eye.

In a sense I look back now with a feeling of sadness when I think of some of my contemporaries. Their mothers would not only make sure that their outfits were the right size, they had to be extremely generous in width and length to allow for growing and with plenty of hem to let down into the bargain! The thirties, of course, produced hard times, and many parents had to be thrifty and far-seeing over such matters.

Of all the attractive windows, none stands out in my mind more than Mrs Kay's wonderful show of the most delicious looking straw hats. Some would be encrusted with white daisies and some decorated with cherries and pretty ribbons and tulle. How I would stand there dreaming, so typical of a little girl, just longing to be grown up in order to wear one of those gorgeous creations!

Denton Street was indeed privileged and much the richer for having these two wonderful shops. They were a credit to the community.

Moving further along the street on the opposite side was dear old Mrs. Potter. Now she ran a newspaper and sweet shop, not forgetting to mention an abundance of toys to suit all age groups, together with games of many descriptions.

Along one side of the shop was a long thick wooden counter on which Mrs Potter displayed her daily newspapers and magazines. On the opposite side was an equally long counter which I could only describe as paradise! No youngsters anywhere could have feasted their eyes on a more wonderful array of sweets and chocolates.

Mrs Potter, a small but wholesome looking lady with greying hair which was tied in a neat bun at the nape of her neck, was as sweet natured as her sugared confections. She was blessed with great tolerance and understanding. A smile comes to my face when I think back to some young characters. They would slowly wander from one end of the counter and back again innumerable times, holding their precious Saturday's penny, just wondering what to choose. This could be a lengthy business, but dear Mrs Potter, the ever-patient lady, would just stand there looking so lovingly at her young customers and wait until they had come to a decision.

How I used to love being sent on an errand to old Ikie Nodder's ironmongers shop! His premises were next door to Mrs Potter. The door bell was so loud it was a wonder it didn't waken the dead!

I think Ikie must have been terribly deaf, as it always seemed like an eternity before he'd make an appearance from his living quarters which were behind the shop. I didn't mind waiting, however, as I simply relished the smell of the place.

Ironmongers shops have always held a fascination for me, but somehow Ikie's was extra special. He was an extremely quiet gentleman, never much chat about him, and could even on occasions be quite abrupt. Perhaps his deafness was a source of irritation to him, who knows. He always managed, however, to produce whatever item Mother required, and it could be assured that nine times out of ten it would be to acquire a 'Brown Betty Teapot!'

There were several fish and chip shops scattered along Denton Street, and trade was always excellent in that direction. Oh yes, Denton Holme people loved their fish and chips! No-one, I might add, enjoyed them more than my dear Dad.

There was Mr and Mrs Dowie's shop which was situated near the Red Arch railway bridge. Mr Dowie was quite renowned in the art of making the most perfect feather-light batter that one could ever have tasted.

Further along the street was Mr and Mrs Becket's shop which was situated close to Mrs Potter's. They were well known for their sales of fried hake and skate as well as cod and haddock. Mrs Becket, who was such a pretty lady with ginger curly hair, always used to have a pan of peas bubbling away in a large pan. These were most popular and sold extremely well.

Although Mr Fred Pieri's shop wasn't in Denton Street, it would seem a shame not to give him an honourable mention. He had a wonderful business which was situated in Northumberland Street. Here again was a man who was a master of his trade and was always known to sell top quality fish and chips. He had two very good looking sons who helped in the business and, together with his extremely charming wife, contributed an excellent service to the public.

Coming closer to home were Freddie and Jenny Renucci.

Their shop, in fact, was next door to ours. They were always most polite, and never failed to whet their customers' appetites by selling pickled onions which were displayed in very large jars. These were sold at five for a penny.

'A twopenny fish and a penn'orth, please Freddie, and plenty of salt and vinegar!' Oh! How those familiar magical words echo in my ears. It doesn't do any harm to wallow in such nostalgia, I suppose. It might do us good, who knows!

The Renucci's children, Freddie and Rita and I were always great friends, and I recall when playing with them in their back yard, frequently going into their large outer workshop to watch dear George Peet laboriously gutting and cleaning box loads of freezing fish. This was quite a messy job, and in order to protect his clothing he wore a large rubber type of apron. A great deal of water was used during this particular operation as the fish had to be meticulously cleaned before being taken into the shop. Indeed, I can still picture George sitting on an old lemonade crate and bending forward to undertake this monotonous and unenviable task.

The potatoes also had to be perfectly prepared, and these were put into a large barrel, the lining of which must have had some sort of grater in order to take off the peelings. George would switch on this contraption and it would proceed to revolve at a fairly fast speed for several minutes. It was quite a miracle to see the potatoes emerge from it looking as though they had been peeled by hand.

Denton Holme was also well equipped with a number of grocery shops, in fact I'm sure everyone was spoilt for choice! There was a somewhat large establishment on the corner of East Nelson Street, which went by the name of 'The Newcastle Tea Company'. What a charming name for a shop! It almost had a Victorian ring to it.

Across the street on the other corner was the Co-op. This particular shop always had sawdust on the floor. One was instantly overpowered by the strong but delicious smell of fresh yeast, an indication that many people must have baked their own bread etc.

A little further along the street, almost opposite Mrs Potter's, was Robinson's very nice grocery shop and Post Office. Hanging from their ceiling were large succulent looking hams and the delicious flitches of bacon for which they were renowned. One could conclude, therefore, that their financial turnover must have excelled in that direction.

Next door to Renucci's fish and chip shop was dear old Mrs Blaylock. Now she must have been in her seventies the way I remember her. She would always wear a black crocheted shawl round her shoulders, and her grey-white hair was of the Victorian cottage loaf style, her large bun being supported by strong looking hairpins and tortoise-shell combs. Seldom was she seen without her black jet beads round her neck and matching brooch on the collar of her blouse, which were doubtless her favourite pieces of jewellery. Whenever Mother sent me to get one or two items from her, I was always somehow relieved when her daughter, Lena, attended to me as she was much quicker and could use the old banger of a hand-turning bacon slicer with greater speed than her mother! Yes, even during the thirties there were some quite primitive pieces of equipment in some of the shops.

Liddy Noble's shop was immediately opposite ours, her window facing into Norfolk Street. Now Liddy was an extremely large and rotund lady, and would stand on her shop door step for many an hour each day. She was so huge that she could be seen as far away as the Red Arch railway bridge. Now that was quite some stretch of street! This particular bridge was removed some years ago. One might have said that dear old Liddy was a landmark, and was always dressed in her familiar long black dress and large white apron which almost reached her terribly swollen ankles.

Despite her twenty stone or more, Liddy had a most appealing kind face with glowing rosy red cheeks. My, but she certainly knew how to bake a good teacake, and her home-made gingerbread was quite excellent.

The hot summers would create havoc with one or two of Liddy's dairy products. Possessing no such cold storage like a fridge, her butter had to be kept as cool as possible by keeping it in a large bowl of cold water on a small lino-covered table. The cheese, sweated like an athlete who had just run a marathon! How worrying it must have been for shopkeepers in those earlier days. Such would be the gamble and the hope of a quick turnover, I suppose.

There were two more grocery shops that I remember. One was owned by Mary and Totsy Riley, and the other by Gertie Ward and her sister. Both shops were situated further along Denton Street and were almost opposite one another. Now these two particular shopkeepers, together with old Annie Dawson who had a shop on the corner of Cumberland Street, were, to my knowledge, the only ones who sold hot pies and peas. These were sold only on a Saturday!

It was quite commonplace to see many a person scurrying along the street carrying a bag of hot pies in one hand and a jug of peas in the other, (own jugs provided!) but doubtless they would be quite delicious and would provide many a household with a cheap and nourishing dinner. Come to think of it, apart from fish and chips, pies and peas must have been the great 'take-aways' of the Thirties!

Denton Street was also blessed with Ida Atkinson's wonderful bread and cake shop. This was situated opposite Ikie Nodder's. How could anyone possibly forget the wonderful aroma coming from her ovens! Oh! Such nostalgia!

My memory takes me back to Mr Bowman's chemist shop. This was on the corner of Graham Street and Denton Street. I recall the day when a couple of workmen, who were putting a new frontage to the shop, were removing some old bottle green tiles. The opportunity to acquire one of these tiles for myself and my young contemporaries simply could not be missed, as they were ideal for the game of hopscotch. We girls in Denton Holme called the game 'itchypot'. We descended on the workmen like a load of vultures! They were so kind, even to the extent of chipping away odd pieces of cement which were stuck to the backs of some of the tiles. Such happy memories!

Next door to Mr Bowman's shop was Mr Frank Astley the Dentist. He was a very caring gentleman, and would always oblige business people who couldn't manage to see him during the day, by remaining open after surgery hours.

There was even a firm of undertakers in Denton Street. This was next door to the Newcastle Tea Company and went by the name of Scriven.

One could hardly fail to see the immense black wooden hoarding with white painted lettering which was fixed to the wall, and read 'Scriven's – Undertakers and Funeral Directors'.

Two brothers, Ronnie and Albert Armstrong, were the only wet fishmongers, and their shop was situated on the corner of Collingwood Street, their main window facing into Denton Street.

Now Albert, the younger brother, was quite a well known celebrity in Carlisle. He was gifted with a most beautiful tenor singing voice, and was known to have taken first place on many occasions at the Carlisle Musical Festival. Indeed, he gave enormous pleasure to many people throughout the County.

I simply must give a mention to James Collins the hairdresser. His shop was a few doors away from ours. Mr Collins was quite elderly, and his own particular hairstyle was quite typical of a Victorian gentleman, straight, with a centre parting, and a large sort of flat curl on either side of his temples. He was assisted in the business by his two sons, Billy and Alf. A long wooden bench completely filled one side of his salon where all his old customers would sit and wait their turn for attention. Many a good crack would take place as old Jimmy could talk the hind legs off a donkey!!

Regarding butchers shops, there were several of them scattered along Denton Street. Oh yes! This was quite a competitive line of business to be in. There was dear John Gavican, whose shop was next door to Ida Atkinson's. Dad and he were such great friends. Diagonally across from John was Ted Simpson's, whilst further along on the corner of Nelson Street was the Co-op Butchery.

Immediately opposite was George Rigg's shop. This gentleman, who was very short and portly, was always affectionately known as Porky Rigg. A couple of minutes walk from Porky's was a shop by the name of Morrow, and lastly there was a business which was situated next door to Armstrong's and traded by the unusual name of 'The Argentine Meat Trading Company'. Locals, of course, always referred to it as 'The Argentine'.

Now no community would be complete without a Public House! The good old 'Prince of Wales' in Denton Street was quite an anchorage, particularly for the older inhabitants who'd meet daily for a beer and a bit of a crack.

How I distinctly remember as a small child, going past the pub on my red painted scooter. I would always stop to watch the charlady scrub the steps. She'd then go over each of them with a pale yellow coloured stone in a squiggly sort of pattern.

The memory of this brings a broad smile to my face! The charlady in question was of very small build with short, straight blackish coloured hair, and she wore dark rimmed spectacles. I somehow didn't think she cared for my presence, and on more than one occasion she'd chase me away, saying that I was a 'layle menace!' Being of curious temperament, I remember going back home one day, carrying this new word in my head and saying to Dad, 'Dad, what does menace mean?' He smiled, asking me why I wanted to know, I innocently replied, 'Well that's what that woman who washes the steps at the 'Prince' says I am!!'

Finally, it is with great pride that I refer to the one and only Rita Irving, whose Dance Studio was in Denton Street. What a dancer! What a teacher! Above all, what a delightful character.

In her younger days Rita was the essence of perfection, her talent and popularity winning a place in the hearts of everyone. Her younger brother, Terry, was positively dynamic, a dancer who performed with great panache. Their dancing displays were sheer magic and never failed to captivate their audiences. They don't make 'em like that anymore!'

Although there were many other shops, one cannot include all of them, but a very important part of Denton Holme which deserves a special mention is its river, the Caldew. Locals, of course, always used to refer to it as the 'Cauder'.

This river gave great pleasure to many people when I was a child, particularly along Holme Head Bay, opposite which was Ferguson's Textile Factory. A huge waterfall which had deep staggering steps was the venue for dozens of swimmers in those wonderful hot summers. They'd dive off these steps into the deep water, swim about for a few minutes, and then arduously climb back up them to do it all over again. There was a long winding set of railings at the side of the bay where bystanders could watch and enjoy the fun and frolics.

I hope I can be forgiven for this, but I always used to chuckle at the style of the swimming costumes which were made of wool, and once they were wet they almost reached the swimmers' knees! How embarrassing and what a drag!! No wonder the extra weight slowed down the climbing process! Still, they were happy times which were a form of escape to many, and all on home ground. Wonderful!

I recall with great sadness during the Thirties when Carlisle had one of its worst storms ever. The river was so high that it swelled its banks, causing hundreds of sheep to be drowned. Bill and I went and stood on one of the bridges to witness these poor creatures being dragged along at high speed, and the pitiful sound of their bleating was most upsetting. This was a most sad and touching scene which I will never forget.

This photograph of my grandmother and her assistant, Miss Pattie Goodger, was taken in 1921, when Carlisle's market was full of character. Note the grape barrels to the right of the picture, now collectors' items!

The Near Boot Inn, Whitecolsegate. In the foreground on the extreme left is my grandfather, together with some friends who were all greyhound enthusiasts. The young boy on the right is my father. Standing in the doorway behind him are his sisters Nan and Clara, whilst in the other doorway are my grandmother and great grandmother.

Willie Kendal, my little self and my beloved Dad.

My grandmother about to take to the skies on the 11th February, 1920. The gentleman seated behind her is Alan Cobham, who would periodically come to Carlisle to entertain with his popular air displays. Enthusiasts could be flown over the city for a fee of five shillings.

This is a most treasured photograph of my dearly beloved mother.

Richardson Street in the 1930s. The tall factory chimney which can be seen smoking away in the background was demolished some years ago.

Mother's little 'steps and stairs', Bill, Hylton and myself.

PICTURE HALL

LEON GOULD'S IMPERIAL PICTURES

This delightful photograph of the Star Picture House is surely a classic. The door at the far end of the foyer led to a Billiard Hall which was extremely popular with men of all ages.

This is the inside of the 'Star' in all its glory. It was the favourite haunt of many people.

The one and only Mary Ann Bowes. One can see that her shop window was filled to capacity, and the daily setting out of her fruit and vegetables was surely evidence of a lot of hard work.

St. James' Annual Church Parade marching along Denton Street about 1925. The band can be seen a few yards behind the delightful old tram.

Another parade marching along Denton Street about 1925. In the background is Ikie Nodder's ironmongery shop.

John and Ethel Beckett, together with their little daughter Joyce, standing in front of their fish and chip shop in Denton Street. The lady to the left was an assistant. The elaborate window decorations, together with their fancy hats, were to celebrate the occasion of the Silver Jubilee in 1935.

Pieri's fish and chip shop. The exotic looking Italian tiles and the style of the range would undoubtedly be quite reminiscent of early models. Note the pans. One would be used for frying the fish and the other for chips. Fred is the gentleman wearing a hat, and his assistant Tom Underwood is seated next to him. The lady on the right is Fred's sister Rosie.

This photograph of Fred and Josse Pieri takes me back to my childhood! The row of old buildings in the background was situated at the back of Junction Street. One of the sections was used to accommodate the pony and trap, whilst another was used for the making of their delicious ice cream for which they were highly renowned.

This group of Rita Irving's young dancers was taken in 1937. I believe the venue was the Crown and Mitre Ballroom.

Loaded up and ready to deliver the goods to the local shops. This was Underwood's Mineral Water Works, which was situated in Junction Street. The building still exists. The business itself was taken over some years ago and now operates from Peter Street, trading as Underwood and McMichael.

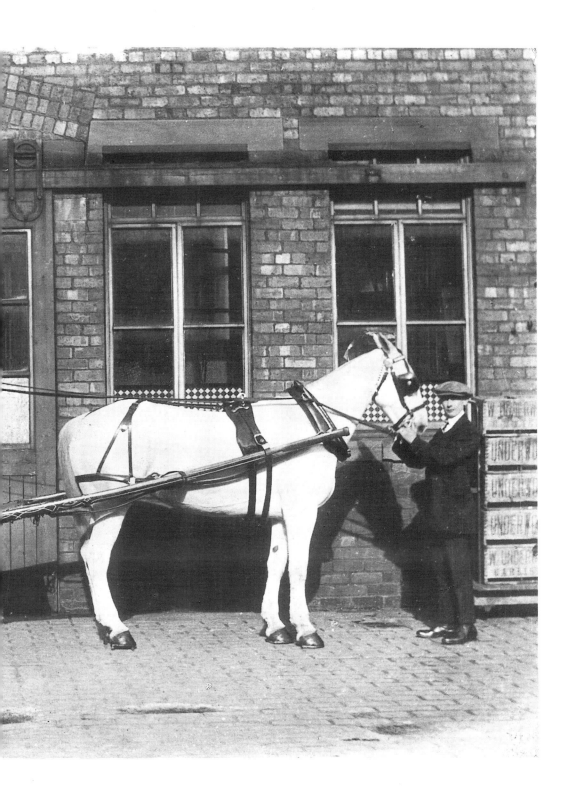

Rita Irving and a group of young members of her dancing school in 1939. The venue for this display was Carlisle's popular Silver Grill's Pageant Hall.

Johnston's grocery shop was situated at the corner of Cumberland Street and Norfolk Street. Although I knew it only as Atherton's in the 1930s, the shop's frontage remained exactly the same. Their house was immediately to the right of the photograph, and being such a friendly child, I would visit the Atherton family quite frequently where they always gave me a very warm welcome.

Denton Crescent was where Mrs Little had her sweet shop. This was situated near the old Red Arch Railway Bridge.

Fargie Johnston, brother of the two ladies with the grocery shop in Cumberland Street, a familiar figure in his day. He is seen here with his knife-grinder, a most intriguing piece of equipment. The elderly lady in the background patiently awaits the return of her carving knife!

Pieri's sweetshop was situated mid-way along Denton Street. The selection of their confections was so wonderful, one was spoilt for choice! The numerous boxes of top quality chocolates with their beautifully decorated lids of satin bows were a sight to behold. Their ice cream was also sold here and was in a class of its own.

Holme Head Bay and Textile Works. The waterfall gave a great deal of pleasure to swimmers and divers during the hot summer months.

Anderson's well known timber yard. Note the railtrack in the forefront. The Red Arch Railway Bridge ran alongside the yard, but was demolished many years ago.

*My dear grandfather. Note the
hairstyle and the waxed moustache.*

*The setting is Robert Ferguson School yard. The three proud pupils are Jack Taylor,
myself, and Norman Steel. The teachers are Mr. Tiffin and Miss Johnstone. As a team of
swimmers, we won the trophy, beating all other schools in Carlisle. What a proud moment
this was, and such an honour for the school.*

This group of hard-working men was taken at the old slaughterhouse, Devonshire Walk, in the 1920s. Note the tools of their trade hanging around their waists – the sheath knives and the steels. This establishment evokes many extremely sensitive childhood memories which sadly, are unforgettable.

St. James' Parish Church reigns majestically over Denton Holme.

This is an earlier photograph of Edmondson's cloggers and boot repair shop somewhere along Denton Street. The exact location is unknown to me.

This grocery shop belonged to the Wheeler family and was situated at the far end of Holme Head Road. The window to the left of the photograph looks into North Street.

A group of youngsters from the St. James' Blencowe Street Mission, celebrating Jubilee Day 1935. A small part of Trafalgar Street can be seen in the background.

The people of Charlotte Street celebrating the end of the 1914-18 war. These houses have sadly now gone and have been replaced by Council flats.

Chapter Four

The Unforgettables

It is so truly amazing when looking back over the distant years how certain people would create an almost indelible impression on one's young mind. One such person was Martha Wilson, a most decorous and charming creature. The more I think of her, she was the epitome of a Victorian character from a Dicken's novel. Her purpose was to deliver milk along Denton Holme.

I suppose it was Martha's appearance which so fascinated me as a child, as she was attired like no other person. She always wore a black blouse with matching skirt which reached to the soles of her feet. Fastened around her waist was a full length coarse apron which protected her skirt from any spillage of milk. A dark woollen shawl would grace her frail-looking shoulders, and never was she seen without her enormous black brimmed hat. Under that hat was the sweetest face, wrinkled with the ravages of time, but so full of character, and one which had so obviously weathered the storms of life.

Every morning, with clockwork regularity, Martha and her two brothers would arrive along Denton Street with their old pony and float. How hard-working and dedicated they were! Deliveries would commence, each separating to attend to their own particular streets.

Martha always carried a heavy looking churn, together with a couple of measures which hung over the side. Jugs of all sizes and shapes would be left on each door-step, some with small cloth covers placed on top to protect the milk from soot and furry four-legged intruders! A more than generous measure could always be guaranteed from this dear lady.

Such methods of delivering this vital household necessity were so primitive, and yet for the likes of Martha and her dear brothers, and indeed many like them, the daily task must have been quite arduous.

I feel privileged to hold the memory of such a quaint, unassuming character as charming as Martha Wilson and, on reflection, what a wonderful subject she would have made for many an artist's canvas!

I have a special abiding memory of a somewhat tragic figure who was known to all and sundry as Dodie. Now this odd looking little man, who was every inch a vagrant, portrayed to me a picture of sadness and loneliness.

Dodie's small feeble frame was clothed with the most ragged and tattered garments that one could possibly imagine, and, whether it was winter or the hottest day of summer, he would always be seen in an old overcoat which had seen many a better day. His old cap seemed to just hang together, its neb almost threadbare and falling apart, whilst his worn-out trousers, which were several sizes too big, were roughly rolled up at the ankles. He wore clanky old clogs, and they never seemed to be fastened – in fact I don't think he possessed any laces.

One was always visually drawn to Dodie's eyes which were red and sore looking, and his face which was always covered in heavy thick stubble. He had sheltered accommodation at Carlisle's old Workhouse, but he was known to frequently jump the wall of the place in order to gain his freedom.

Each day he could be seen walking along Denton Street, and then he'd sit on the stone flags under Liddy Noble's shop window. Few people ever spoke to him, and poor old Dodie would just sit there in silence with his own thoughts and drearily watch the world go by. Liddy would eventually come out of her shop and sharply request him to move on. He'd immediately get up and slowly walk away, at the same time making sure that his old tin can, probably his only possession, was safely secured in his torn overcoat pocket.

This down-and-out itinerant little beggar was known to knock on doors and plead for something to eat. 'And hev yu a droppu tea for uz Maggie?' he would ask. Those were the only words he was ever known to utter.

Although this little man had nothing in the world, his image is worthy of remembrance, for after all, though clothed in rags and tatters, he was, as my dear Mother used to say, someone's son, and above all a child of God. May his soul forever abide with his maker in perfect love, joy and peace.

There was one particular character who stands out in my memory, a young chap by the rather odd nickname of Pump. He'd come along Denton Street every afternoon selling numerous copies of the Evening News. He was a very popular young man and always had a nice word for everyone.

As a small girl, I used to be fascinated with his dark frizzy-looking hair which hung down over his forehead. His cap was worn right back on his head which seemed to frame his appealing looking face. His complexion was somewhat ruddy, due no doubt to his outdoor life in all sorts of weather, and his eyes were dark and most expressive. I can almost see him now, his coat tails flapping about in the breeze, whilst in one arm he carried his newspapers. His free hand was always in his pocket jingling his coins.

After traipsing up and down the street, Pump would come into our shop and hand us a copy. He always enjoyed a quick word or two, never failing to quote the latest headlines. He'd then end his late afternoon stint by standing beside the lamp-post outside the shop, where numerous people seemed to appear from nowhere.

Very sadly, this poor dear lad was killed during the early part of the War whilst on active service. We were, in our household, so terribly upset as this untimely end could not have happened to a nicer and more popular person.

From sadness to a little bit of hilarity! Before referring to the next well-known character, I feel I ought to explain that Dad acquired some of the very latest equipment in order to make pork pies, and he employed an excellent pastry cook by the name of Les Todd. They sold exceedingly well which pleased Dad immensely.

Now one old dear in particular, Johnny Routledge was his name, would habitually call at the shop for a free pie. He was of slight build, I recall, and his dark brown cap which seemed to be several sizes too big, would be worn well over his face, the protruding neb creating a dark shadow. Who knows, perhaps it was to detract from his over-sized nose of which he was sensitively aware.

Sadly, Johnny's frequent calls were becoming a bit menacing. He would stand in the shop scoffing away, and then, as if glued to the floor, would remain there for almost an hour at a time. Dad became so totally fed up with this daily occurrence and decided to dish out a few harsh hints, but all to no avail. The little man simply would not budge! A solution, however, to dispel this frequent visitor, and one which Dad thought would sicken Johnny of his pies for ever, was to add an excessive amount of pepper to the next one. Cruel though this was, and very much against Mother's will, Dad, in desperation, proceeded with the plan.

So-be-it, the next morning Johnny arrived as usual, whereupon Dad handed him the well-seasoned pie. Awaiting his reaction and confident that this daily ritual was about to come to an abrupt end, Johnny turned towards Dad, his eyes by now filling with water, said … 'Well, Geordie lad, that's the best pie yet! There's nowt layke a good bitta pepper tu keep tha cauld oot!'

There was no answer to the problem, Mother suggesting to Dad that it was perhaps best to accept it all as part of life's rich tapestry!

I used to be greatly fascinated by a rather nice gentleman and his wife – I never knew their names – who regularly came along Denton Street with what I would term as a mobile workshop. They performed an excellent service to all the butchers by sharpening their knives and choppers.

This contraption, which was pushed on wheels and was deep green in colour, had a stone wheel which went round and round at the touch of a foot pedal. The speed of this ingenious piece of machinery would cause the knives to throw off sparks as they were being sharpened. This was done by the gentleman, whilst his wife collected the knives etc. and then returned them to the shopkeepers as soon as the work was completed. They were a very reserved couple and so well mannered, and Dad always took pleasure in dealing with them.

This small handful of characters who were extremely well known, and who indeed portrayed different shades of colour into our lives, must surely qualify as Denton Holme's unforgettable of the Thirties.

Chapter Five

More Reflections

The acute awareness of poverty prevailed in so many families in the early thirties. The depression caused so much misery, and it was quite commonplace to see men, and sometimes women, wearily pushing along the street a well-worn wheelbarrow containing coal. I think it was called nutty slack. This was acquired from an old railway yard which was situated near the Red Arch at the far end of Denton Street. I believe the coal was much cheaper to buy that way, and poorer families had no option but to obtain it in this manner.

How harassed these poor dears looked, and some would be occasionally compelled to stop to rest their weary arms and to catch their breath. It can't have been much fun pushing home such heavy loads, but no doubt at the end of the day their efforts would be rewarded with the warmth of a crackling fire.

How can one ever blot out such memories as these without realising and appreciating how lucky and privileged my brothers and I were to have had parents who provided us with such homely comfort. This was life as I saw it through my own young eyes.

The familiar sound of heavy clogs would echo along Denton Street early each morning. Mother would be giving us all breakfast when we'd hear the workers making their way to the factories. Some would whistle, some would chat, and the odd person would quickly stop beside our windowsill and stroke Kitty, our little black cat, who'd be waiting patiently to come indoors after sleeping outside all night. 'Let's clap Mrs Cullen's cat for luck', they'd say.

Being so small, I used to wonder where everyone came from, and did they earn a lot of money. Were some of them dads, I remember asking Mother, and did they love their little girls and boys like Dad and she loved us. Such an enquiring child I was! I suppose in a way the majority of them would be just too glad to be earning a wage, however meagre, as jobs were like gold during the depression.

Groups of men, some very shabbily dressed, would congregate each dinner time across the street at the corner of Liddy Noble's shop. Young and middle-aged, they'd all get together for a chin-wag. They must have felt totally inadequate and bored stiff with their mundane existence. One old dear, Clogger Graham, so called for obvious reasons, and who had his shop a couple of doors away from Liddy's, would leave his tools at the same time every day to join in the chat. I often used to wonder what they talked about!

Now 'Clogger' was a great character and much loved by everyone. Being somewhat portly and fairly tall in stature, he would always wear extremely loud-checked clothes and sport a very jaunty brown bowler hat. A large ragged looking moustache seemed to dominate his face and, to complete the picture, a larger than average pipe would be stuck between his strong looking teeth. He was, in fact, what Dad used to call 'a right old timer', always straightforward in manner and called a spade a spade.

All our shoes were repaired by old Clogger, and one particular day Bill and I were sent to collect Dad's shoes. We used to love going into his shop, as he had so many interesting tools, and of course we could always manage to ask him a million questions!

'Hey Clogger', Bill would enquire, 'wat du yu dee wid this auld tinnu muddy watter?' Clogger would look somewhat sternly over his old spectacles which were placed near the end of his nose.

'Well A'll tell yu wat Aa dee wid it,' he said, 'Aa sawk the leather in it tu soften it afoor sheppun' it tu the shoe, it meks it easier for uz tu work wid."

'And Clogger', Bill would continue, 'wat du yu fill yer mouth up wid aw them nails for?'

'Tu save us gan into that box ower theeur aw the tayme, that's wat Aa dee it for', he'd reply.

Realising that he was going to be in for a barrage of questions, Clogger decided to cut short the encounter!

'Noo look you two', he said, beginning to get a bit ruffled. 'A'll give yu yer fatha's shoes an' yu can git yersels away yem. A've ed enough u yer questions. Aa needn't wrap them up, yuv awnly across the street tu gan, and afoor Aa forgit, tell yer fatha A've put an extra bitta leather on the saydes, it'll 'elp tu thraw 'im ower a bit.'

What a great character Clogger was! I can still picture him sitting at the side of his window, his bowler hat resting on the back of his head, his mouth full of nails and hammering away on his last. Yes indeed, nostalgia can be quite a powerful drug!

It is with great affection that I call to mind what one might have regarded as a weekly ritual. Each Saturday morning, two nuns, who were clothed in full length black habit, would call at our shop. Being of an extremely generous nature, Dad would give them a wrapping of sausages and meat, together with some meaty bones to make soup or broth for the orphaned children of Nazareth House. A sixpenny piece was also included to help along their much needed funds. These dedicated ladies always looked so radiant and their gratitude was expressed in their beautiful smiles. After giving Dad a blessing, they would then leave the shop and put their parcels into an awaiting black van.

Most Saturday nights after closing the shop, Dad would get a large metal tray containing an assortment of pigs' trotters and sausages and the odd bits of meat which would undoubtedly have lost its bloom over the weekend, and he'd take it to the Model Lodging House in Lowther Street. These items were handed in to the Supervisor to be cooked for the less fortunate old men of the city. Such was Dad's generous heart, always thinking of those less fortunate than himself.

I can even recall one Christmas Day when Mother roasted an enormous turkey. Before sitting down to partake of the festivities, Dad carved a complete half of the bird and took it to the 'Model' as it was commonly called. This beautiful gesture most surely symbolised Dad's generosity.

When I look back on Dad's way of life as a butcher and all who were in the meat trade, each had to go to the Auction Mart every Monday morning. This was situated down Botchergate, an area south of the city. Each trader would look over the cattle, sheep and pigs, then sit in the auction ring in readiness for the bidding to commence and hope to acquire the particular beast previously selected. Arrangements would thereafter be made to have the stock conveyed to the slaughterhouse, which in those days was situated a short distance from Carlisle Castle.

The trend is so much different today, as it appears to be the practice for many butchers, but not all, to simply lift up the telephone and order from the local Meat Company a couple of forequarters of beef or whatever they require to suit their needs, and then await its delivery. I feel I might be forgiven if I sound somewhat prejudiced, but the butchers like Dad and others of his day were what I would term as 'good all-rounders', capable of selecting top quality stock and also able to slaughter.

Each Monday after attending the auction mart, Grandfather Cullen would always return home with Dad for a late lunch which consisted of a plate of cold roast beef with lashings of mustard and bread and butter. After the meal was over, he would habitually sit in front of the fire awaiting Mother to perform her weekly task, that of trimming his waxed moustache! This was an ordeal of which she was not at all enamoured, but nevertheless carried it out each time with pleasing results! Despite the fact that Aunts Bess, Nan or Clara could have undertaken this delicate operation, his preference was always for Mother as he thought she was so meticulous. He was without a doubt an exceedingly handsome man, and his appearance, which was so important to him, was always impeccable.

My love for my grandfather was very deep. I always knew that when he'd sit me on his knee with his arms around me, telling me that I was more precious to him than all the treasures in the world, that he meant every word. His love made me feel secure, and when he passed away some years later, a great void was left in my life.

The number of times I used to frequent the slaughterhouse with Dad was numerous. Now it would be quite wrong of me to blame him for taking me to such a place. Indeed, I so loved being with him, and to have a ride in the van around town was quite an event as I always took a keen interest in everything that was going on around me.

Invariably Dad would make a number of business calls and deliveries and, despite his forewarning that he had, of necessity, to drop in at the slaughterhouse, it made not a scrap of difference, there was no holding me back! As time went by, however, I gradually kept thinking of those poor animals until I became obsessed by their sadly awaited fate. The sight of the bullocks being forcibly led into the particular booths to be shot, the pungent smell of the blood, and watching the slaughtermen cut off the hides of the poor wretched creatures, has remained vividly on my mind to this day, a mental scar which will never heal.

I regret with my whole heart witnessing such slaughter at a tender and impressionable age. I would give anything to obliterate from my mind this particular part of my childhood, but what is done, I fear, is done, and I can only but point the blame in my own direction.

Living in an atmosphere where the unavoidable smell of meat seemed to be all that we ever breathed, some might have regarded it as therapeutic, but as far as I was concerned, it didn't do anything for me! I used to positively hate Thursdays when Mother had to make the beef dripping. The fat would be rendered down in one of our large boilers in the workshop and, even though a very large window was always left open in order to let out the vapour, somehow the pungent smell would seep through the cracks of the door which led into our living quarters.

Another thing that was really quite soul destroying was the wretched sawdust which Dad scattered on the shop floor. This, of course, was very necessary in all butchers' establishments, in fact it was compulsory, and anyone not adhering to this rule could be in serious trouble from the Sanitary Authorities. However much we wiped our feet, the horrid stuff always managed to trail throughout the house. This highly offended Mother as well as making extremely hard work for her.

Having a good business was one thing, but behind the scenes life was not exactly a bed of roses! I so often wondered why Dad chose to be a butcher in the first place. Surely he could have chosen an easier way to earn a living! I suppose, however, it was the done thing in those days that a son would automatically follow in his father's footsteps.

The chances of Hylton carrying on with the family tradition in the years to come were indeed extremely slim! In no way did he intend to become engrossed in a way of life so mundane, and especially when he showed no signs of interest. He was by now attending Grosvenor College in Carlisle, a private school for boys, which was situated in Chatsworth Square. Hylton had a wonderful brain and, with respect, his ambitions far exceeded those of the butcher's block! Bill and I, of course, were a little younger, and our thoughts at that time were naturally directed to childish matters with no consideration whatsoever of what we would like to do when grown up.

There was one family tradition which Mother insisted would not be broken, her expressed wish being that I learned to play the piano. So-be-it, from the age of seven I was tutored by a Mr Arthur Ryecroft who lived a couple of minutes away from our house. He was an excellent teacher, very patient and with a gentle approach which suited me down to the ground.

Once I mastered the keyboard, it was a case of practising scales for evermore! I certainly at that time didn't lack enthusiasm, in fact I progressed quite rapidly. This, of course, delighted Mother, and my efforts well surpassed her expectations in view of the fact that I was so young.

Now these lessons took place once a week after getting out of school, but there were one or two occasions when I simply didn't wish to attend. This attitude did not please Mother in the least, and she was quite bothered in case I was losing interest. There was no accounting for my inexcusable behaviour! Well, before one could say 'knife', an envelope was pushed through our letterbox, the contents of which contained a few harsh words both of annoyance and disgust from Mr Ryecroft. He hastened to point out that his wife had lit a fire in the parlour especially for my benefit, and the fact that I was becoming somewhat unreliable was a sheer waste of coal. The note ended abruptly, the writer stating that he could not tolerate the whims of a child, and had therefore decided to terminate my tuition forthwith! I must say that I was truly sorry for my flippant behaviour, and felt ashamed that I had humiliated Mother by letting her down so badly as well as upsetting Mr Ryecroft.

Within a few short weeks, Mother managed to find a new tutor for me, a most charming lady by the name of Mrs Cairns. She, too, was an excellent teacher, and these lessons continued for a further six years, Mother making sure that there was no repetition of any hanky-panky!

In retrospect, I shall always be grateful to Mother for giving me the chance and encouraging me to study music, for there are times, when feeling a little downcast, that the tinkling of the ivories swiftly clears away the dark clouds in my head and produces a rejuvenated attitude to life.

The pattern of life in Denton Street was always unpredictable. Each day would bring something different, and some particular happenings seem to stand out in one's memory more than others.

It seems almost like yesterday when Bill and I were playing outside the shop. We were chasing each other round and round the old silver painted lamp-post, thoroughly enjoying ourselves. We were so excitable and noisy that Dad was compelled to leave his customers for a few seconds and come outside to reprimand us. His stinging words of rebuke soon had us scurrying back indoors to Mother. Just as he was turning round to go back into the shop a rather nasty accident occurred, when a gentleman, who was driving a very large car, collided with a young cyclist. The young man had unfortunately caught the tyres of his bicycle in the tramlines. Dad saw the whole incident and immediately ran into the street to give his aid to the badly shaken youth.

The usual crowds had by this time congregated, and then the police arrived on the scene. Being a key witness, Dad was asked to give evidence, and this he did accordingly. It was ultimately decided that the driver of the car was not at fault, but the cyclist's misfortune to have steered his bicycle between the said tramlines.

A few days later, the gentleman who drove the car called at the shop to see Dad and to thank him for his help in the matter. it turned out that he was none other than Mr Howard Carrick who owned the Hat Factory in Norfolk Street. He cordially invited Dad to go along to the factory to be specially fitted for a hat. What a delightful gesture, Dad thought.

The measuring and fitting duly took place, and within a few days a most wonderful looking box was delivered from the factory. Such excitement prevailed, and I remember Dad handing it to his little darling and allowing me to do the honours and take off the lid. Well, what a hat! Dad was absolutely thrilled to bits; it was an Anthony Eden Homburg in a most perfect shade of grey. How distinguished he looked, and although I say it myself, he always looked so gentlemanly when attired in his best garb.

The following Saturday night, Dad put on his best suit, plus, of course, his latest acquisition, and went with some friends to a pub at Cummersdale, a small village not more than three miles or so away. Duly placing his hat carefully on a peg, he and his friends wandered through to the Bar. Drinks would no doubt have been consumed, although Dad never indulged very much as he suffered rather badly from a stomach ulcer. He simply enjoyed a good chat with his friends, and besides, a little change from the grindstone didn't do any harm.

Getting ready to return home, he went to collect his hat, but alas, it was no more! Some sick joker had taken a pair of scissors and completely cut off the rim!

Such sacrilege, Mother thought, when Dad showed her the result of this needless and wilful destruction by some ignorant, stupid idiot.

This elegant piece of head gear, this token gift so unexpected, was most surely short-lived! Oh indeed, for the unforeseen happenings of life!

Well now, from hats to fridges! I would like to refer to the fridge which was in the back workshop. This really was a monstrosity! Unfortunately, Hylton, Bill and I occupied the extremely large bedroom which was situated immediately above. Every hour or so the motor in the fridge would make the most rumbustious noise, it was like Hell let loose!

This dreadful din would go on and off continuously, which I suppose was more pronounced with the stillness of the night. Through the day it was perhaps not as noticeable, with the bustle of life going on all around. How we used to curse the wretched thing, in fact a perfect night's sleep was quite foreign to us! Dad, of course, would gently point out that if he didn't have the fridge, then he wouldn't be able to run the business!

Once or twice each week we used to have deliveries of enormous blocks of ice which were placed into large grids inside the fridge. These blocks were brought on a horse-drawn flat wagon by two workmen, who were known as 'ice men'. In order to carry out this thankless task they were equipped with thick leather jerkins, almost like that of a coalman, plus a large piece of coarse sacking which hung down their backs. I imagine that when they lifted these heavy blocks with their strong ice-picks, the sacking would give them a better grip.

Ice men indeed, it must have taken them hours to thaw out at the end of each day, poor things, and one cannot help wondering if they ended up with rheumatism in their old age. No doubt someone had to do this particular job, and if it provided them with a wage, then I suppose they'd be just too glad to do it.

With the passing of time, engineering skills progressed to more up-to-date machinery, and Dad, like many other butchers, bought the very latest equipment, thereby dispensing with the monotonous ice delivering ritual.

I must say that our bedroom was extremely pretty. Hylton and Bill slept in a handsome brass bed. Mine, too, was brass, but a single one. The quilts on both our beds were absolutely gorgeous. These were made by Mrs Groggins, a dear lady who lived in Cumberland Street. The walls displayed the most beautiful tapestry texts, and all were worked by Grandmother Hodson. The mantelpiece was white with a charming ornate black cast iron inset. Indeed, the room was always cosy looking and welcoming.

Mother even cultivated the most delightful looking window-box imaginable, so that we could enjoy looking out on an array of colourful flowers. The reward and pleasure from her efforts, however, was sadly to be short-lived. On pulling back the curtains one morning, the ubiquitous Darky – that huge black cat belonging to Annie Blair, lay fast asleep in total oblivion, intoxicated by the warmth of the morning sun, thus flattening the whole creation! So much for having a lower kitchen roof whereby the said offender could gain easy access to our windowsill! All hope of success was ultimately abandoned, as there and then Mother realised that to persevere with such a project would be a complete waste of time!

How could I ever possibly forget one particular night when Mother put us to bed. She kissed us goodnight, as always, and like most children, we promised to behave ourselves and get to sleep. Our promises, however, were like pie crusts!

To put Mother off the scene, Hylton commenced to sing. He had a voice as sweet as any choirboy. We managed to remain as fresh and wide awake as a bright Spring morning, when at last, the awaited moment had arrived to pursue our plan of action! A pillow fight had been planned, and Hylton, who was always the instigator of such events, delegated me to keep watch at the door in case Mother should come upstairs for something or other. What happened in the next few minutes was certainly not envisaged by my darling brothers. Hylton's pillow burst, and within seconds the room was showered with an abundance of feathers. What a fiasco!

Undoubtedly filled with a generous measure of adrenalin and declaring himself the victor of this wild frolic, Hylton proceeded to jump vigorously up and down on the bed. The ensuing moments were quite catastrophic! Sounding as though the heavens had opened, this beautiful bed which Mother treasured, came crashing to the ground, its fittings having come apart. Such total devastation had to be seen to be believed, but one can rest assured that the outcome of this naughty escapade did not pass without regret.

Dad dealt with us in no uncertain terms and made us pay the penalty for the mischief caused! Hylton was banned from going to Houghton for a week, whilst Bill and I were not allowed to go out and play with our friends for the same length of time.

Indeed this lesson, this punishment, most surely disciplined us, Dad's methods proving to be a great deterrent in the event of any further misbehaviour!

It is inevitable when one looks back at one's childhood that one laughs at certain memories. This little episode which I am about to relate is one which simply must be told.

Bill and I were playing together in the yard on this particular morning, when dear Miss Robinson, whose house was next door to Annie Blair's, asked us if we would like to do an errand for her. She handed me a small package which was neatly tied with a piece of string. Apparently it contained her brother Billy's sandwiches which he had forgotten to take with him to his work. He was working outside the Prince of Wales pub, digging up the cobbles in the street, she told us.

Feeling most important, Bill and I went along the street to find that there were four men working on the job, one with a drill, another with a pick-axe and two with shovels. We just stood there in total bewilderment, not knowing which of them was Billy Robinson, as, strangely enough, we had never actually seen him before. We never thought to ask, and the sandwiches, we concluded, simply hadn't to fall into the wrong hands! Like a flash of lightning, we went back to Miss Robinson's and knocked on the door. She was quite astonished when she saw that I still had the parcel in my hand.

'Does he have thick string tied round his knees?.' I enquired. 'And does he have a face like this?' I innocently screwed up my face to one side as best I could and kept it like that so that she could have a good look. Miss Robinson instantly roared with laughter, and with a loving gesture she bent down and patted me gently on the head.

'Yes little one', she said, her eyes filling with tears at my comical expression, 'that's my Billy to be sure.'

Bill and I went off once again and duly carried out our small assignation, this time with complete success!

Mother continued her full and busy life looking after us all. There was always plenty of washing and ironing to be done, as well as her helping Dad in the business. I never seem to recall her sitting still and relaxing, and as for cooking, she was never done, poor dear.

With little chance of respite away from the mundane chores, Mother's only pleasure was to visit Grandmother Hodson each Sunday afternoon. Dad would take us to Etterby Terrace in the car, where Mother and I would stay until our return home in the evening. Hylton and Bill, of course, would be taken to Houghton to visit Grandmother and Grandfather Cullen.

I always enjoyed my visits to Grandmother Hodson's, the atmosphere was so bright, and one could always sense a loving welcome. I used to love the coziness of the house with its highly polished Victorian and Georgian furniture and shelves displaying the finest pieces of porcelain. Grandmother had several beautiful clocks, all of which chimed with the sweetest of tones, adding an air of mellowness and peace to the lovely old house. Some of the furniture, incidentally, is in my proud possession to this very day.

These Sunday afternoon visits were very sadly to come to an abrupt end. My dear Grandmother became seriously ill with a nasty bout of influenza. Mother and I stayed with her. There was one particular neighbour, a Mrs George, who came to help in any way she could.

It is somewhat amazing how I can remember this lady. Her rather odd appearance must have created a big impression on my mind at the time, and I can still visualise her walking sprightly up the deep stairs to Grandmother's bedroom. She was quite small, and wore a sleeveless wrap-around pinafore of floral design, doubtless to keep her clothes clean, but the most striking memory of her was the comical looking brown hat which resembled an upturned flower pot! This seemed to tower above her short feeble looking frame. But why, oh why, I wondered, did she keep the thing on in the house?

Being so young and impressionable, I suppose one's little mind would quite naturally be filled with childish thoughts and perplexities and, who knows, being so inquisitive and forthright, I may even have enquired of Mrs George why indeed she never took off her funny looking hat!

With an air of gloom prevailing after a further visit from her doctor, Grandmother's heart had drastically weakened overnight and she was by now in a deep sleep. Mother was gently prepared for the worst.

Quietly tip-toeing down the stairs, I followed Mother into the parlour where she played on the piano a beautiful hymn, 'What a Friend We Have in Jesus'. She sang with such tenderness, her sweet voice breaking with emotion, but it was doubtful if Grandmother ever heard her. As a tiny bystander, and not quite understanding what it was all about, I remember putting my arms around Mother and reaching to kiss her tear-stained face.

The following day, my dear Grandmother Hodson, who in her time had given enormous pleasure to so many with her musical talent, and whose illness was so brief, passed away peacefully.

Amidst her grief, and realising only too well that she had lost her greatest friend, Mother was left with no alternative but to attend to the many business matters which had concerned Grandmother.

The tenancy of the Market stall was immediately terminated, and was promptly taken over by a very dear family friend, a Miss Hannah Hargreaves. This must have been terribly sad for Mother, as it was the end of an extremely successful family business. With all the work she had to do at home, she realised that there was no way she could have continued with the running of the stall and adding to her responsibilities.

Many a tear was shed by Mother for some considerable time, and there were many occasions when Bill and I would come home after playing with our friends, to find her wiping her eyes. We would both hug her so tightly, expressing our love and comforting her as best we could. The threads of life, she realised, had to be picked up again, and so, with a brave heart and bearing her sorry with fortitude, pulled herself together and continued with her busy life.

As the months went by, and with the legal matters settled, Mother inherited everything of Grandmother's, including her properties which were scattered around town. She was now, for the first time in her life, a lady of comfortable means.

Who was it, I wonder, who said we should never look back! Surely life would be rather empty without our memories, even though some are laced with sadness.

Chapter Six

Schooldays

It has many times been said that schooldays are one's happiest. How I respectfully beg to differ with such sentiments! There were many occasions when Bill and I simply dreaded going to school. An almost Victorian-like strictness prevailed in so many of the classes, and even now I can almost hear the echoes of some of the teachers' powerful voices reverberating around the old classrooms. There were, in fact, times when I used to think they were totally devoid of all feeling. Such attitudes did not encourage learning, in my opinion, and in consequence, the inability to concentrate, through fear, created a slower measure of progress, particularly for those pupils who were of a nervous or worrying disposition.

How clearly I remember the numerous occasions when Bill dreaded maths lessons. His teacher, whose name I shall refrain from mentioning, seemed to delight in pulling his ears unmercifully until they ached and ached. Although maths was obviously not one of Bill's better subjects, such inclement treatment was quite uncalled for.

This same teacher fell down the stone steps of the Robert Ferguson School one day, badly injuring himself, when one of the boys came running across the school yard and shouted to Bill and a few of his classmates, 'Ev yu hurd the latest, lads! Auld … uz fell down the steps and brocken 'is leg.'

'Brocken 'is leg', chirped up one of the lads, ' 'e should uv brocken 'is bloody neck!'

How sad, in retrospect, that such remarks were made! Surely this teacher's attitude, had it been a little more human, would have created harmony and understanding between himself and those less fortunate pupils who found difficulty in grasping certain subjects, and would, therefore, have caused less fear and misery. Above all else, they might even have acquired a true liking for him!

I recall one particularly unsavoury occasion when I was a pupil at Morley Street Junior School. A girl, who had been given a sixpenny piece in order to do some shopping for her mother, sadly lost the coin. Quite naturally, being worried, she reported the matter to the teacher, a small middle-aged lady, who was extremely slender, and with tightly permed grey hair. It appeared that we were all instantly put under suspicion.

'Lift up your desk lids', she said, her eyes glaring strictly at each one of us. We were then asked to search through each other's books and pencil cases for the missing coin. The sordid crunch came when we were asked to take off some of our garments, including our shoes and stockings. Young as we were, this sort of treatment was utterly appalling! Why indeed did we have to undergo such indignation, and why did the teacher jump to such an instant conclusion that the wretched coin had been stolen! The girl in question could have mislaid it or, indeed, have lost it anywhere.

The miserable affair which was such a humiliating ordeal, was to be endured for some considerable time. The school bell rang as usual, which of course was the indication that lessons were over for the day. To our utter dismay, none of us was allowed to go home until the coin was found. We sat there in silence with our hands clasped on our heads, some pupils extremely tearful and longing to go home.

'You'll all sit there until someone comes forward with the coin', remarked the teacher looking at us so sternly.

The time had reached five o'clock, and I recollect hearing the voices of a few mothers who must have undoubtedly been worried, and who had arrived to take their loved ones home. They waited patiently in the large cloakroom which was adjacent to our classroom.

A great darkness came over the sky, followed by thunder and lightning. We were all, by now, so terribly frightened. The thunder, which was as loud as a thousand beating drums, was mild in comparison to the ensuing moments. Into the classroom walked my dear Father like a raging bull. I can almost feel my face heating up all over again whilst recalling this miserable episode. Within the following sixty seconds, everyone headed for the door like a flock of frightened sheep. This teacher was given a polite mouthful in no uncertain terms. Dad literally didn't miss her and hit the wall! The missing sixpence, I would add, was never found!

Now since ever I was able to scribble, the habitual use of placing a pencil or crayon in my left hand was, to me, quite a natural phenomenon. After all, the good Lord blessed me with two hands, and I'm sure He held no hard and fast rules as to which one He preferred me to use!

Shortly after being upgraded to a more advanced class, my sewing teacher, noticing that the needle was in my left hand and that I was stitching from left to right, very sharply took me to one side. Most emphatically she insisted that I commence placing the needle in my right hand and proceed to sew from the right. I was totally bewildered by this, and her determination to make me alter my ways was quite soul destroying.

I was complete shattered, and no longer was this particular subject a pleasure to me, but one of total distress and tribulation. Each subsequent lesson was approached with fear, and the thought of being shown up in class for my misfortune did nothing to help matters.

As the weeks went by, it was evident to Mother and Dad that something was bothering me, and most certainly I wasn't the happy and carefree child that I was of late. A slightly nervous stammer began to develop and this, quite naturally, was causing them great concern. I began to tell them what had been going on at school and how I could no longer endure this torture. By now I was completely overwhelmed and I wept profusely.

Without a moment to spare, and by now full of fury, Dad took me by the hand and marched me to school. Such was his eagerness to get this extremely cruel and intolerable injustice put to right, he forgot to remove his white butcher's overall!

After a few forthright deliberations which were not to be ignored, this teacher was left shaking in her shoes! The happy prospect of being able to sew once again with my left hand was sheer bliss, in fact I was completely rejuvenated!

I was so grateful to Dad for coming to my aid in my moment of need and, once again, he proved to be my greatest ally.

On reflections, this teacher, whose aim to alter nature's way, quite rightly did not succeed, her only achievement being my needless misery!

Whilst Bill was a great sprinter and had won numerous medals, I found that swimming was my own personal forte.

I was chosen as part of a small team of three, to take part in a swimming competition at Carlisle's Swimming Baths. My other two young contemporaries were Norman

Steel and Jackie Taylor. Now all the schools in the City entered their best teams in this prestigious event and, although it was not a race, it was to decide which team had both the best style as well as speed. Imagine our delight when Norman, Jackie and I were acclaimed the winners. A photograph of we three jubilant youngsters duly appeared in the Cumberland News, and for the first time in my life I felt that I had achieved something worthwhile!

To strike another colourful note, General Elections and Local Elections always accorded us a day off school. Indeed, what could have been better!

These particular occasions provided us with an opportunity to indulge in a bit of innocent fun, each of us being equipped with a home-made object which consisted of lots of newspaper tightly wrapped to form a type of parcel. This would then be tied with string or twine with an extra couple of yards or so in length, including a loop at the end to accommodate one's hand. Now these pieces of nonsense were called 'Red and Yellas' or 'Blues and Yellas'. Red represented the Labour Party, yellow the Conservatives, and blue the Liberals. Their purpose was to hit each other on the head in the event of answering one's young assailants with opposing party colours.

'Are yu rid or are yu yella?' would be the threatening question of the day. I might add that one had to apprehend certain young characters with great caution and, although a lot of fun was derived, there would undoubtedly be a few headaches at the end of the day!

Whether or not this particular bit of nonsense was indigenous to the youngsters of this dear old City of Carlisle, I simply wouldn't know, nor would I know if the tradition still prevails. Perhaps with the passing of time it has just melted away.

One particular highlight in our school calendar, was the preparation of the Silver Jubilee celebrations of our beloved King George V and Queen Mary.

To mark this very special occasion, a dazzling programme of events was to take place at Brunton Park, Carlisle's well-known Sports Ground, where most children from the various schools in Carlisle were to participate.

Now one particular item which was quite the most outstanding spectacle of the day, involved hundreds of boys and girls to form a tableau of the Union Jack which was to cover every inch of this vast ground. In order to do this, each child was issued with either red, white or blue berets, together with matching jumpers.

I always remember Bill's outfit was red and mine was royal blue. We were all to march neatly on to the pitch from different angles, each section of colour contributing towards the design of the flag. Once we were in position, we all had to crouch down, showing off our respective colours to great advantage. I can almost hear all over again the crowds cheering at the tops of their voices at this spectacular sight, it must have been absolutely dazzling.

A large brass band accompanied us in the singing of so many of our National songs. These were rehearsed for weeks, and at the very last singing lesson at school Bill was asked to stand in front of everyone for not knowing the words of Land of Hope and Glory.

'You will write out each verse three times, William Cullen', said the mistress in charge, 'and bring the evidence of your writing to me first thing in the morning.'
Poor Bill, I thought, and what a boring task he would have ahead of him when getting home from school. He ought, of course, to have known the words and could only but blame himself for landing in such a predicament.

After returning home from school that afternoon, we duly changed into our playing clothes, as was the practise, and then had tea, Mother asking us the usual questions about our lessons, I, of course, was bursting to tell her about Bill and the singing rehearsal, when suddenly I felt a foot gently kick my ankle. Well now, if ever there was a look of 'don't spill the beans', it was surely written on Bill's face! There must be a reason, I thought, why Mother wasn't to hear about the incident. Call it intuition if you like, but minutes later I was to discover that I was to fall victim of Bill's shortcomings!

'Gan on Babs', he said, putting his arm around my neck, 'be a sport and write the bloomin' words for uz'. 'Aw gan on', he continued, the expression in his big brown eyes absolutely pulling at my heart strings.

'A'll give yu a ha'penny if yull dee it', he said in earnest.

'Oh all right', I replied, his face lighting up with apparent relief. 'But you still won't know the words by the morning', I said anxiously, 'and what about Miss Gaddes, she'll just about kill you and I'll worry.;

'Aw naw she won't', replied Bill with a huge smile on his lovely face. 'Besides', he continued, 'tomorru is the big day at Brunton Park, and the auld lass won't ev tayme to bother aboot me, will she?'

Knowing that I was doing wrong and realising that Bill ought to pay for his own mistakes, I fulfilled his request, and with no thoughts in my head about the ha'penny! You see, my love for him was so deep, and no matter what he asked me to do for him, I did with a never ending love. Mind you, I have to admit that to a small girl, the lyrics of the song in question were a total bore. Why, oh why, couldn't they have been something like 'You Made Me Love You', they would have been much better don't you think!

The many street parties which took place to celebrate this momentous occasion will always bring back stirring memories. Cumberland Street in particular was absolutely magnificent. Everyone decorated their parlour windows in red, white and blue crepe paper, some displaying pictures of the King and Queen, whilst a profusion of colourful bunting fluttered so proudly in the gentle breeze from one end of the street to the other.

A large table made from trestles was placed down the middle of the old cobbled street, and on either side were wooden benches to accommodate dozens of children.

I remember turning the corner from Norfolk Street into Cumberland Street and walking rather shyly along, when a lady, I can't recall who she was, said, 'Come on Babsy love, sit on here.' and she gently lifted me over one of the benches. There seemed to be so much love shown to one another in those days.

The almost despairing Thirties did not alter people's affections, no matter what their circumstances. The people of Denton Holme were, without doubt, the salt of the earth.

Well, what a great party this was! There was everything imaginable to eat, including sandwiches, colourful iced buns, jelly and as much lemonade as we could drink. We were each given a paper hat and a balloon, and streamers were thrust nonchalantly in the air and across the tables. What tremendous fun we had!

Close beside me sat my dear friend, Madge Lapping, whilst Bill sat further along with her brother Cyril and Jack Stainton. There must have been about a hundred children sitting around this massive party table, which made such a wonderful change from sitting behind school desks!

Some of the more elderly people in the street sat on old kitchen chairs outside their front doors, lovingly watching their very young contemporaries enjoying this truly momentous occasion.

This huge gathering of happy youngsters watched by their mothers and dads, uncles and aunts, grandparents and friends, joined in the fun and excitement of this unforgettable day, and in all innocence no-one dreamed that within a few short years this beloved country of ours would be at war with Germany.

Chapter Seven

The Dark Clouds of War

The war brought great changes to all our lives, many families with loved ones having to leave home to join the Forces.

Although Hylton was on the brink of a promising career, he shelved his plans to become a land agent and surveyor and immediately volunteered for the Army. Up to that moment he was serving his articles with the County Land Agent, Mr. Arthur Gibson, and was doing incredibly well. He always was, of course, extremely studious and ambitious, even as a schoolboy. To do his bit for his country was all that mattered to him, and he was just one of the many young men whose ambitions had to be set aside.

Even shopkeepers' lives were terribly disrupted, especially food shops and, with the introduction of rationing, much chaos was caused behind the scenes. This extra work, which entailed a great deal of writing, fell on Mother's shoulders. All customers' names and addresses were entered in a large book, with a special note of the number of persons in each household. Coupons were then cut from their ration books and, after being carefully counted, were sent at regular intervals to the Ministry of Food Department. What a performance! Meat, of course, was allocated accordingly, and as for someone living alone, rations were truly quite meagre.

Dad had by now acquired a second shop which was situated in the Market Entrance, Scotch Street, in the centre of town. His success was instant, hard graft rewarding him with an excellent clientele. Consequently, Mother had a double dose of paperwork to do!

How I used to be so sorry for her looking after the Denton Street shop, especially during the winter months. The freezing cold atmosphere made her mouth swell up beyond all proportion and caused her sweet face to look completely distorted. I simply don't know how she endured it, poor darling. Handling freezing cold meat all day long, and with no heating in the shop was, to me, quite barbaric! I remember how the customers would come to the shop and sympathise with her, but Mother always managed to put on a brave smile and say that it would soon be on the mend. Her beautiful nature was exemplary.

Each Friday morning at the unearthly hour of half past four, Mother and Dad were busy putting up everyone's rations. This was a job of great precision. I can still hear Dad using the chopper on the block, needless to say that the noise reverberated round all the upstairs rooms. Bill and I, however, had only one thought in our minds, and that was for Mother's well-being as she was so fragile looking.

As soon as this work was done, Dad would have a quick breakfast, and then he'd dash to the other shop and do exactly the same thing, getting everyone's rations ready. Indeed, life was quite hectic in the Cullen household.

Bill and I had by now left Robert Ferguson School and were attending Grosvenor College and Wykeham House School respectively.

My weekends away from school always accorded me the time to do as much of the housework as possible, and as long as it lightened Mother's heavy burden, then that was all that mattered.

One particular Saturday after getting the grocery shopping done, Mother sent me along to Kay's shop for a navy blue hat. They were so kind and understanding, realising that Mother couldn't leave the shop, they put five hats in a large box for her to try on. Service with a smile was so typical of the Kays, such charming and obliging people. On reflection, Mother must have been so terribly frustrated with her life, all work and very little play.

The war continued, and presented a portrait of sad times, as hardly a week would pass without someone losing a loved one. Denton Holme people were always especially sympathetic, always ready to help and share each other's sorrows. Perhaps a young soldier would be home on embarkation leave, enjoying a few days of freedom, and then weeks later he'd be killed in action. Laughter and tears have always been close companions.

As time went by Hylton transferred from the Army to the R.A.F. and within a few short months, after strenuous training, he became a night fighter pilot.

Like all families, we used to delight in him coming home on leave. Hylton always used to send a telegram to Dad at the Market Entrance shop, saying what time he'd arrive. The shop was full on that particular morning of 28th March 1942, when the excitedly awaited telegram arrived. Alas, it was stated with deep sorrow, that Sergeant Pilot Hylton George Cullen had been killed during the early hours of that morning. He had been engaged on operations the night before. It emerged that my beloved brother was almost back to his base when his plane went into an air pocket. He bailed out of the plane, but tragically his parachute failed to open.

Like many other families throughout the country who had lost their loved ones, we were all in deep shock, and trying to come to terms with the situation took a very long time to accept. Poor Mother, she especially must have been terribly grieved to think that over the years she had lost two of her darling children. Hylton was within a few weeks of celebrating his twenty-first birthday. Indeed, he was little more than a boy, and should have been with us longer than fate decreed.

As soon as he was eighteen, Bill joined the Army. The wrench was terrible, as he and I were always so close. We always declared that we'd never marry, and that one day we would live together in a cottage and keep a parrot!

The time had come when Dad made the big decision to sell up and leave Denton Holme. All three properties, which included the shop and two houses, were bought by our dear friends next door, Freddie and Jenny Renucci. It was, for them, an opportunity to expand their property.

We moved to Brampton Road, and the transition from living in a bustling environment to one of comparative peace took some getting used to! One has to say that it was almost like living in Paradise, waking up to the sweet sound of tiny birds chirping in the trees.

The thoughts of Mother being released at long last of her miserable existence, were of tremendous relief and sheer joy, but how terribly sad to think that she had given up the best years of her younger life before being set free. Thirteen years, after all, was a long time to be more or less imprisoned in a freezing cold shop. No-one, in my eyes, had a more sweet, unassuming and loving Mother.

Much water has passed under the bridge since those days. Very sadly, my darling Bill met his fate at the early age of forty-one, a cruel and tragic blow which shattered us all. My beloved Mother and Dad passed away some years later.

As surely as there is a time to rejoice, there is also a time to be sad, from which there is no escape, and how ever heavily sorrow weighs, one has to take a grip and courageously ride out the storms of life. I am richly blessed with treasured memories of my loved ones and of my childhood in Denton Holme.

GLOSSARY

Aa	I
aboot	about
afoor	before
an'	and
anywez	anyway
Aw	Oh
	(also all)
Awnly	only
bitta	bit of
brocken	broken
claym	climb
dawn't	don't
dee	do
divvel	devil
doon	down
durrty	dirty
'eed	head
fatha's	father's
gan	go/going
git	get
hev	have
hing	hang
hurd	heard
iv'ry	every
knaw	know
lang	long
layke	like
luv	love
meks	makes
mooth	mouth
naw	no

nee	no
nivver	never
noo	now
nut	not
oor	our
oot	out
ower	over
pawl	pole
raustin'	roasting
sawk	soak
saydes	sides
sheppun'	shaping
tayme	time
tek	take
theeur	there
thraw	throw
tu	to
upsayde	upside
uz	me
warrlick	warlock
watter	water
watt's	what's
weel	well
wesh	wash
wunder	wonder
yem	home
yersells	yourselves
yis	yes
yit	yet
yu	you
yud	you would